Stop Stumbling Over Yourself

Dr. Ruby J. Harvey

Stop Stumbling Over Yourself

Charleston, SC
www.PalmettoPublishing.com

Stop Stumbling Over Yourself
Copyright © 2022 by Dr. Ruby J. Harvey

All rights reserved

No portion of this book may be reproduced, stored in a retrieval system, or transmitted in any form by any means–electronic, mechanical, photocopy, recording, or other–except for brief quotations in printed reviews, without prior permission of the author.

Scriptures are from the KJV Bible

First Edition

Paperback ISBN: 979-8-88590-663-0
eBook ISBN: 979-8-88590-664-7

Contents

Introduction	1
Negative Thinking and Speaking about Yourself	9
The Island Mentality	23
Putting Up Walls to Block Others Out	31
Controlling Our Emotions on Purpose	37
The Journey of Fear	45
Internalizing Your Problems Can Make You Sick	47
Conclusion	51

Acknowledgments

I am so grateful to the Lord Jesus Christ for empowering me to write this book. I give Him all the glory for the things He has done! I would like to thank my husband, District Elder L. J. Harvey, for his support and encouragement through this project. Thank you to all of my supportive family and friends who helped me to mold this book in order to help those that it will bless.

Introduction

What is stumbling over yourself? It simply means you are a hindrance to yourself. It means that you allow your weaknesses, your actions, and your personal shortcomings to stunt or stop your growth. You are, in your own way, stopping your own self from moving forward. We can stumble over ourselves mentally, emotionally, spiritually, and even socially. Sometimes the problem is not others; it's us. *Stop Stumbling over Yourself* is an invitation for growth and a reminder that in order to get where we need to be in life, we have to take responsibility for our actions, attitude, outlook, and overall life.

Bad things happen to all people here and there in our lives. It doesn't matter what family you come from, how much money you have, or your status in life; trouble finds everyone sooner or later. Job 14:1 says (King James Version) that "man that is born of a woman is of few days, and full of trouble." Verse 2 says, "He cometh forth like a flower, and is cut down." The book of Job is a good example of the story of Job's life of suffering, revealing to us how a person should stand in the midst of his troubles and trust the Lord to bring him through his situation, no matter how bad it is. Job passed the test with God. The book of Job begins by telling his story. To list a few things about him:

1. He was perfect and upright.
2. He feared God and he shunned evil.
3. He suffered very much in his life.

The story tells us that God gave the devil permission to attack Job. He lost all of his children, servants, cattle, and all other animals in one day. Job's response to his great loss can be found in verses 21 and 22. He says, "'Naked came I out of my mother's womb, and naked shall I return thither: the Lord gave, and the Lord hath taken away; blessed be the name of the Lord.' In all this Job sinned not, nor charged God foolishly."

The story of Job shows us that everyone suffers, but we decide how we will respond to it. There may not be a lot of people like Job that handle their situations the way Job did. Many of our troubles are not as extreme as his, but sometimes it may be hard for us to go through them. One thing about Job is that he took responsibility for his life. He did not try to hide or throw in the towel; neither did he blame the Lord or anyone else. In Job 2:9–10, his wife says to him, "Doth thou still retain thine integrity? Curse God and die." But he said unto her, 'Thou speakest as one of the foolish women speaketh. What? Shall we receive good at the hand of God, and shall we not receive evil?' In all this did not Job sin with his lips."

The Word of God tells us: "All that live godly in Christ Jesus shall suffer persecution" (2 Tim. 3:12). As the people of God, we must have faith and believe in the Lord for all things. Heb. 11:6 says, "But without faith it is impossible to please him: for he that cometh to God must believe that he is, and that he is a rewarder of them that diligently seek him." In the blessed times and in the times that we don't feel so blessed, whatever the situation is, we must learn to maintain our integrity and not handle our problems in anger, bitterness, and blaming others (Eph. 4:31-32).

I heard a pastor say once that Job and Joseph suffered more than most people in the Bible, and yet neither one of them let God down, from the beginning until the end of their stories. They both were rewarded in the end because their responses to their troubles pleased the Lord. If the Lord allows us to suffer in any situation,

He'll be with us. We can be responsible and trust Him to bring us out. When we get angry, fight back, and make excuses, we're stumbling over ourselves. In order for us to get through this life, we must grow up, learn what the Lord is saying to us, and be willing to follow Him in all things.

Rom. 14:13 states, "Let us not therefore judge one another anymore: but rather, that no man put a stumbling block or an occasion to fall in his brother's way." We should never decide what's right for other people nor stand in their way, because the Lord is the judge of us all. Here's what you need to be concerned about: that you don't get in the way of someone else, making life more difficult than it already is.

Wikipedia defines *stumbling block* as a metaphor for a behavior or attitude that leads to sin or destructive behavior. According to this definition, we can be a stumbling block to other people and hinder their progress, which is not pleasing to the Lord. We must also understand that in actuality we can be a stumbling block to our own selves. It's easy to point the blame at others, but we can be our own worst enemy.

As we grew up in life, went through elementary school, graduated high school, and perhaps went to college and/or trade schools, we learned many different things that prepared us for life. We also experienced a lot of negative things. Some of us grew up and matured, while some of us grew and did not mature as much as we should have. We will clash with others sometimes because we're not like them. When we don't grow and mature as we should, many of us become selfish, mean, hateful, bitter, revengeful, and unforgiving. It's sad to say, but many of us have become bullies just because we couldn't have our way. If you don't like who you are in life, you have the opportunity to change what you don't like about yourself and strive to become the best person you can be. It can start by loving yourself, learning how to manage yourself, caring about how you look and how you present yourself to others, and attending to your attitude when you're not in complete control of yourself.

We want to stop stumbling over ourselves by learning how to turn our thinking around from negative to positive. Phil. 4:8 states: "Finally, brethren, whatsoever things are true, whatsoever things are honest, whatsoever things are just, whatsoever things are pure, whatsoever things are lovely, whatsoever things are of good report; if there be any virtue, and if there be any praise, think on these things."

Negative Thinking and Speaking about Yourself

From my experience of growing up, I went through a lot of negative things in school and in life. I really didn't know how to handle the things I went through. I learned later that everything I had suffered in life from my childhood until adulthood molded me into a certain kind of person with a certain kind of behavior.

I didn't become mean and hateful, but I still didn't know what to do with the pain that I carried inside. What I learned to do was keep silent about it since I didn't know who to share these things with. I knew I could potentially make things worse by talking to the wrong people.

We need to have counselors and trusted friends around us to help us make good decisions because sometimes when troubles arise, we don't always know how to handle them. The truth is we're not failures because we don't always know what to do. As believers, the first thing we must learn to do is honor God in every situation. Prov. 3:6 says, "In all thy ways acknowledge him, and he shall direct thy paths." I noticed that this scripture ends in *paths*, showing us that we will always have different roads to travel, different journeys to take in life. We must learn to seek God in all things, no matter where we are in life. He will send the answer to your spirit or through a person or a dream—somehow, He will reveal Himself to you. If we honor Him by honoring His Word, He'll answer us and always be on time. Remember Daniel: he fasted and prayed for twenty-one days, and the answer to his prayers was sent the first day but was held up by the enemy called the prince of the kingdom of Persia. In Dan. 10:12, the Lord revealed to Daniel, "Fear not, Daniel, for from the first day that thou didst set thine heart to understand, and to chasten thyself before thy God, thy words were heard, and I come for thy words." We will have many challenges in life, and we should always consult the Lord our God on His direction through every situation. Even when He doesn't answer right away, remember your faith is being tried.

There are different kinds of situations and troubles that we all suffer in this life. At this point in life, I have discovered that the Lord Himself will help us. When you've tried everything and everything has failed, turn to Jesus.

He'll help us; He'll fix our problems and heal us from our sicknesses, diseases, and problems. We just have to put our trust in Him. Rom. 8:28 says, "And we know that all things work together for good to them that love God, to them who are the called according to his purpose." When you're in a difficult situation, you can't always see things clearly, nor do you understand it at the time, but you must believe that all things are working for your good.

Joseph is an example of standing on the Word of God in his negative situations. Throughout his trials he suffered much pain and ridicule, yet he never spoke or thought negatively about his problems, and in the end, God delivered him and promoted him. It was God's plan for him all the time.

The story of Joseph shows great sufferings in this young man's life. He was next to the youngest of twelve children. His father, Jacob, whose name God later changed to Israel, had four wives. Joseph's mother was named Rachel, and she died giving birth to his younger brother Benjamin. As Joseph was nourished by his father, he grew up as a young man with great integrity, and his father loved him. Gen. 37:3 says, "Now Israel loved Joseph more than all his children, because he was the son of his old age: and he made him a coat of many colors." The story of Joseph is covered in Gen. 37–50.

Looking at the life of Joseph helps us to understand that we do not have to let the things we go through change us or cause us to behave in an unseemly manner. We don't have to retaliate because things don't go our way. Things will go wrong, and many times we will clash with other people. This is a part of growing up in the world. Just know that you're not a failure when or if you discover that some people don't like you without cause.

Some things about Joseph:

1. His father loved him and made him a coat of many colors (Gen. 37:3).
2. He was a dreamer; his dreams came true later in his life (Gen. 41:42–44).
3. His brothers hated him for his dreams and for his words (Gen. 37:9).
4. His brothers became angry with him because he showed up in the fields where they worked. Joseph's brothers told their father that Joseph had died when they had thrown him in the pit and sold him to the Egyptians.
5. He was falsely accused of rape at his master's house and went to prison for this crime he did not commit (Gen. 39:11–19).
6. Joseph was promoted in Egypt. A famine fell in Egypt, and Joseph was the only one that could instruct the pharaoh of Egypt on what to do, so he promoted Joseph in his kingdom, second to himself.

Everyone honored Joseph for his wisdom and knowledge of knowing how to feed the people in the famine.

7. Now the truth is about to unfold because Joseph is not dead; he will now serve everyone in the land because of a famine. Pharaoh promoted him and put him in charge of dispensing food to the neighboring lands, including his father's house and his mean brothers. Pharaoh put a ring on his finger and made him the greatest person in the land next to himself. All of Egypt honored Joseph.

8. In the end Joseph hugged his brothers, cried, and forgave them. He served them food, as he fed the surrounding lands, and brought Jacob and the family to Egypt to live.

When we examine Joseph's life of suffering and all the bad things that he went through, we see it wasn't for nothing; God had a plan for his life.

Joseph followed after the things his father had taught him about the Lord and everything concerning what was right and the right things to do. Joseph's life of suffering worked out for his good and for the good of the people. Because he stood on his faith and processed the good things his father had taught him, he survived everything negative that came upon him. Rom. 8:28 shows us that there is a purpose for us in life and that we must continue to fight to win rather than fight ourselves by retaliating and making all kinds of excuses. When we do the opposite of what is right for ourselves, we will keep stumbling over ourselves in life.

Remember, everything doesn't have to be a problem for us. We can learn how to cast away negative things that happen to us. If we don't, the negative things will follow us through life, and we'll always be trying to fight people, get even, threaten others, and dismiss people. In order for us not to stumble over ourselves, we will have to take personal responsibility for all of our actions and reactions to our problems. It's important that we be the best example we can be. When we put on our best behavior, we're showing others the right way. We're letting our light shine before men so they can see our good works and glorify our Father who is in Heaven (Matt. 5:16). When we do the opposite of what is right, we're not stumbling over anyone else but rather have put a stumbling block in our own way—we are stumbling over ourselves. This behavior is not good for our lives. We should never think negative thoughts about ourselves because there will be enough enemies for us to fight in the world; we shouldn't be an enemy to ourselves. Whatever we think about ourselves, that's who we will become. As Prov. 23:7 says, "For as he thinketh in his heart, so is he."

We can look back on the life of Joseph and examine how some of us act and react to situations in comparison to the way he chose to respond in his negative situations. This lesson shows us that we can't fight these battles alone. As Jesus says in John 15:5, "Without me ye can do nothing." You might notice in life that what gets a lot of us into trouble is our responses to the negative things we experience with other people.

Often we fall back into our old patterns of life, and our thoughts, words, actions, and feelings get out of control. In order for things to change, we must start thinking about where we are in life and desire to be the best we can be. I heard a statement once that said, "Your gifts can take you places your attitude can't keep you." Since our gifts and attitudes work together for our success, we will be the ultimate reason behind whether we rise or fall.

One reason we should take responsibility for our actions and stop stumbling over ourselves is that other negative people will have enough to say to put you down. If we don't learn to be responsible for our actions, we will continue to get into trouble. We should strive to change and realize that we are valuable to the Lord and He can help us through this life. In Luke 4:18, Jesus shows us that He came to save the poor, to heal the brokenhearted, to preach deliverance to the captives, to restore sight to the blind, and to set at liberty those who are bruised. Jesus loves us so much that He wants us to know He's always available to help us, wherever needed. He gives us the invitation to come to Him when He says in Matt. 11:28–30, "Come unto me, all ye that labor and are heavy laden, and I will give you rest. Take my yoke upon you, and learn of me; for I am meek and lowly in heart: and ye shall find rest unto your souls. For my yoke is easy, and my burden is light." Jesus is assuring us that

He can and will help us if we just come to Him and ask for His help. He has it all: salvation, healing, and the power to make us completely free. Everything starts in the mind in Christ Jesus. Phil. 2:5 says, "Let this mind be in you which was also in Christ Jesus." We will not automatically have the mind of Christ, but we learn as we read and study the Word of God. When we allow the Lord to help us, the positive attitudes enter in. That's when people will begin to see our value, and we will be able to be in a position to help others.

Negative behavior will cause people to avoid us and not want to be around us. We must always remember that everyone is not like us and that all of us have a backstory that has molded us in certain ways. When we remember this, it helps each of us to learn how to cope and coexist in this world, even when dealing with people who are stumbling blocks to themselves and who don't take responsibility for their actions. When we are healed, we can help others.

Putting It All Together:

1. What are some things you can do to start making your life more peaceful?
2. What changes can be made to be more responsible?
3. If you change your thoughts, what else changes?
4. What was Joseph's attitude in his sufferings?
5. When he didn't respond to hatred, what was holding him together?
6. How many times did he speak negatively about himself?

The Island Mentality

When we come to a place in our lives where we feel we just need to get away from everyone that troubles us and all the things that are in our way, we often isolate. Wikipedia has a couple of descriptions of the island mentality. This is the one that I would like to mention: "The term 'island mentality' is also used in some psychological research to describe individuals who dislike or have problems with relating to others, and then live as loners or 'islands.'" Wikipedia goes on to say that people with this mentality "may feel inferior, afraid, or alone." The island mentality consists of thoughts like:

1. I need to get away from all these people who are trying to run my life.
2. People are always trying to tell me what to do.
3. Most of these people don't like me for who I am.
4. I'm tired of being bothered, so I'm going to pull myself away.

It's not healthy thinking to desire to cut yourself off from people who love you. We must not only learn to exist in this world but also learn how to coexist with other people, whether they are in your family, at your job, or in your neighborhood.

I'm reminded of a man in the Bible named Jonah. He was called by God to go and preach to a great city named Nineveh and to cry against it for their wickedness against God. He understood the message, but instead of obeying it, he immediately ran away to Tarshish. He decided not to go because the people of Nineveh were very evil and displeasing to the Lord. But as we know, the Lord is a loving God, and scripture tells us, "The Lord is not slack concerning His promises, as some men count slackness: but is longsuffering to us-ward, not willing that any should perish, but that all should come to repentance" (2 Pet. 3:9). As Jonah thought on his assignment that the Lord had given him to go and preach to Nineveh, he decided that he would not do what the Lord had asked him to do. He ran away and got on a ship that would take him far away from his assignment. The story goes on to tell us that Jonah went down to Joppa, paid his fare, and boarded a ship to take him to Tarshish, far from the presence of the Lord. After this, the Lord sent out a great wind into the sea, so that the ship would be broken. After Jonah got on, the ship began to have problems, and the other passengers on the ship figured out that the trouble didn't start until Jonah got on the ship. Jonah was down in the sides of the ship asleep. The men confronted him for putting them in harm's way all because he wanted to run from God. The men threw Jonah off the ship, and God created a big fish to swallow him. He stayed in the fish's belly for three days and prayed to the Lord. Not only did the Lord hear him, but He also gave him the assignment again. Jonah went to Nineveh to preach this time, and he cried out against the city of Nineveh. They became sorrowful for their wickedness and fasted and prayed for three days without food or drink. The Lord forgave them, but Jonah got angry because the Lord forgave the city of Nineveh for their great wickedness.

Your situation may not be as bad as Jonah's, but if you refuse help from people who are able to help you and think that separating yourself is the answer, then you are running away. We can blame other people and make as many excuses as we can, but the truth of the matter is we are stumbling over ourselves. It's time to shake yourself and get up and speak healing and forgiveness into your life. It's time to declare that you will have the victory. You are important to the Lord God, and there are some people you are important to as well. You don't have to isolate and separate yourself.

The passage 1 Cor. 12:12–27 says,

> For as the body is one, and hath many members, and all the members of that one body, being many, are one body: so also is Christ. For by one Spirit are we all baptized into one body, whether we be Jews or Gentiles, whether we be bond or free; and have been all made to drink into one Spirit. For the body is not one member, but many. If the foot shall say, "Because I

am not the hand, I am not of the body"; is it therefore not of the body? And if the ear shall say, "Because I am not the eye, I am not of the body"; is it therefore not of the body? If the whole body were an eye, where were the hearing? If the whole were hearing, where were the smelling? But now hath God set the members every one of them in the body, as it hath pleased him. And if they were all one member, where were the body? But now are they many members, yet but one body. And the eye cannot say unto the hand, "I have no need of thee": nor again the head to the feet, "I have no need of you." Nay, much more those members of the body, which seem to be more feeble, are necessary: and those members of the body, which we think to be less honorable, upon these we bestow more abundant honor; and our uncomely parts have more abundant comeliness. For our comely parts have no need: but God hath tempered the body together, having given more abundant honor to that part which lacked. That there should be no schism in the body; but that the members should have the same care one for another. And whether one member suffer, all the members suffer with it; or one member be honored, all the members rejoice with it. Now ye are the body of Christ, and members in particular.

You don't have to go about thinking you are in this alone. You don't have to live with an island mentality.

Putting It All Together:

1. Do you believe having an island mentality is the answer to solving your problems?
2. Is any aspect of your desire to be alone rooted in bitterness or unforgiveness?
3. How can opening yourself up to others enrich your life?

Putting Up Walls to Block Others Out

Sometimes there can be positive effects just to clearing your mind and going away for a while to reset for life. Whether it's because of a troublesome job, family issues, or difficult relationships, sometimes you may just need to take a break for a little while. But if there comes a time when you want to escape permanently and put up walls, you're not helping yourself; you're actually stumbling over yourself, and that's not a safe place.

Sometimes we put labels on ourselves like:

1. **I'm a loner and have always been this way.** Some of us have said this because we thought life would be so much easier if we didn't have to deal with people. A few years ago, someone said to me, "I could live my life better if it wasn't for people." But the truth is that if we think like this, we will always be defeated. When the Lord God created the universe, He put people in it. I've heard the saying, "We're a work in progress." We are definitely a work in progress. We are all still growing and should allow others to do so without judging them or putting up walls.
2. **I love being alone.** This is most likely not the truth. The truth is that being alone will keep us from receiving the help we could receive if we had friends or mature, competent people to talk to sometimes.

3. **I really don't have to listen to anyone else.** We must realize that we don't know it all and that there is always someone who can impart knowledge and wisdom on us. Prov. 12:15 says, "The way of a fool is right in his own eyes, but he that hearkeneth unto counsel is wise."
4. **There are too many enemies against me.** When we feel that we have too many enemies, it will cause us to distrust everyone, even those who are actually able to help us.

Some other thoughts and emotions that show us when we have walls up:

1. Repeatedly rehearsing past experiences
2. Fearing change
3. Dealing with unforgiveness and practicing unforgiveness
4. Not understanding that walls can affect future relationships

Putting up walls hides our true selves, and as long as we keep up the walls, we'll never be free to see things the way they are. The walls are not there to protect you; they are there to destroy you and keep you stumbling over yourself and blaming other people.

Why do we put walls up by not allowing others into our lives? One reason could be that we have not dealt with our brokenness and are in need of healing. When Jesus was on earth, He healed all that came to Him. Matt. 8:16–17 says, "When the even was come, they brought unto him many that were possessed with devils: and he cast out the spirits with his word, and healed all that were sick: that it might be fulfilled which was spoken by Esaias the prophet, saying, 'Himself took our infirmities, and bare our sicknesses.'" Jesus is the answer to all of our problems, no matter what they are, be it physical, mental, or emotional pain. When we feel any of these discomforts, the answer is not putting up walls—this is not the way to healing. The Lord healed and delivered all that came to Him. I know He did because I believe what is written, and I also know by my own experience and healing through the Word of God. We are the only ones that can make this madness stop. Once we learn to let go of bitterness, unforgiveness, and resentment, and let down the walls we have put up to keep others out, we will see that our lives will become better and more fulfilling. Eph. 4:32 says, "And be ye kind one to another, tenderhearted, forgiving one another, even as God for Christ's sake hath forgiven you."

Putting up walls will cause unnecessary struggles for you in life. There is help available for you, but you must be willing to receive it. That help can come in many different forms: family, friends, pastors, and counselors, but most importantly, God. Just be sure to always seek God regarding what to accept into your life when you let down your walls—always be discerning in all your decisions. Start the process of healing and positive thinking. When we are experiencing any kind of behavior that causes us to harm ourselves and hinders us from progressing in life, the answer is never putting up walls. I remember in past times, I put up my own personal walls because I didn't know how to handle the pain and injury I had received, even from childhood until now. The time has come for us to stop fighting ourselves and being our own enemy.

Putting It All Together:

1. What have I experienced in life that has caused me to put up walls?
2. How can putting up walls hinder me?
3. In what ways will my life benefit if I let my walls down?

Controlling Our Emotions on Purpose

We should never allow negative emotions to control us. Negative emotions are connected to not being responsible for our actions. References from www.verywellmind.com state that basically, negative emotions are there to alert us that something needs to change. Since we know and understand that these negative emotions are there to alert us that some things need to change, we need to take action by paying attention to these signs and working to change the negative things in our lives. Many people have been able to make a change by changing the way they think about themselves.

They began to think on these things:

1. "I'm better than this; I believe in myself." And they arose and began to renew their thoughts to turn things around.
2. "I've been stumbling over myself, so this day I'm going to stop my old ways of thinking in order to start afresh." This is the first step on our path toward healing.
3. "I want to stop being my own enemy, but I don't believe I have the strength to do it on my own."

Change always hurts, but when we decide to take that first step, there is help in Jesus. We can trust the process of changing because the Word of the Lord says, in Jer. 29:11, "For I know the thoughts that I think toward you, saith the Lord, thoughts of peace, and not of evil, to give you an expected end." Also, Isa.41:10 states, "Fear thou not; for I am with thee: be not dismayed; for I am thy God: I will strengthen thee; yea, I will help thee; yea, I will uphold thee with the right hand of my righteousness."

Regardless of what happens to us and what people think about us, it doesn't matter because God's got us! He said, "I know the plans I have for you," and He said, "Fear not; for I am with you." When there is a plan of God and when we believe and have faith in His Word, it's only a matter of time before it shall come to pass. I know this for a fact because it has worked in my life so many times. Many times, people get tired of going through the same things in life, but if you don't quit, you will experience the victory and gain your own testimony of what the Lord can and will do for you if you let Him. We must be willing to cancel out every thought that will hinder us or cripple our lives. We can't function and live a normal life when we continue to cling to our own ways by stumbling over ourselves.

Everyone has dealt with some kind of situation in life that has affected their emotions. I'm reminded of the story of Moses. Pharaoh, the king of Egypt, sent out an order to kill all of the baby boys. Moses's mother told his sister Miriam to hide him in a basket in the river. Moses was found by Pharaoh's daughter, who took him out of the river and raised him as her own son. She taught him the Egyptian ways, but that was not who he was. Heb. 11:24–26 says, "By faith Moses, when he was come to years, refused to be called the son of Pharaoh's daughter; choosing rather to suffer afflictions with the people of God than to enjoy the pleasures of sin for a season; esteeming the reproach of Christ greater riches than the treasures in Egypt: for he had respect unto the recompense of the reward." One day, he went out where his own people were and saw an Egyptian beating a Hebrew, one of his own people. He killed the Egyptian and hid him in the sand. He took an opportunity to jump in to defend his brother, but the outcome wasn't good for him. Not only was he the son of Pharaoh's daughter, but he was also a murderer and a fugitive because he ran away. Moses had many obstacles in his life, but God had a plan for Moses's life. No matter how bad his life was or what people's opinion of him was, the Lord chose Moses to be the one to deliver His people from bondage. The story of God calling him to go to Pharaoh and tell him to "let my people go" is found in Exodus, chapters 3 and 4).

Some of the excuses Moses made when the Lord met him to give him the assignment were:

1. I'm not important enough. (Exod. 3:11)
2. What shall I say? (Exod. 3:13)
3. They will not believe me. (Exod. 4:1)
4. I am not a good speaker. (Exod. 4:10)
5. Please send someone else. (Exod. 4:13)

Moses ran away from his problems literally, but sometimes we run away and avoid our problems emotionally. Because certain things happen to us in life, we develop insecurities and make excuses. This example of Moses reminds me of some of my past negative actions and reactions and the excuses I would make to support what I wouldn't try to do.

Moses stumbled over himself until he arranged with God how he would go. All of Moses's excuses angered the Lord (Exod. 4:14). Sometimes the Lord has to use other people because some of us refuse to take action and come out of hiding. Remember: it's never too late! When Moses ran away after killing that Egyptian, he was forty years old; when the Lord sent him back on his assignment, he was eighty years old.

Putting It All Together:

1. Why is it important not to fear?
2. Why should we pay attention to God's plan? (Jer. 29:11)
3. What are some things that we can do to control our emotions on purpose?

The Journey of Fear

When I was a child, there were times I felt all alone with a situation that I didn't know what to do with; it was very frightening. Sometimes, as adults, it's easy to feel fearful. Life can make us feel like Dorothy in *The Wizard of Oz* when they were in the woods: "Lions and tigers and bears, oh my!" Even as we try to face our fears with faith, it seems that more devastating things happen to us. Even in the midst of things that cause fear, we must have faith until we make it to a place of comfort and peace. Ps. 56:3–4 says, "What time I am afraid, I will trust in thee. In God I will praise his word, in God I have put my trust; I will not fear what flesh can do unto me." Whatever state we find ourselves in, we must learn to think positive thoughts to keep fear out of our reach.

Fear can cause torment and can spiritually cripple you and handicap you, causing you not to function the way you need to. Just remember, fear is not the spirit that God gave to the believer. As stated in 2 Tim. 1:7, "For God hath not given us the spirit of fear; but of power, and of love, and of a sound mind."

Putting It All Together:

1. What are some ways that we can conquer fear and get it out of our lives?
2. How would you recognize fear if it showed up?

Internalizing Your Problems Can Make You Sick

Keeping a lot of things inside and not being able to release the pain we carry from negative incidents is not healthy or good for us. It's called internalizing your problems, and by holding in negative thoughts and feelings, eventually you will become sick with things like high blood pressure, diabetes, ulcers, mental issues, and, worst-case scenario, a nervous breakdown.

I have personally experienced internalizing problems, and I know that you can become sick with some of these things. I turned to the Lord for help, and He immediately showed me in the Word of God how to think and process my thoughts and be released from these bondages. John 8:36 says, "If the Son therefore shall make you free, ye shall be free indeed." In Luke 4:18, Jesus says, "The Spirit of the Lord is upon me, because he hath anointed me to preach the gospel to the poor; he hath sent me to heal the brokenhearted, to preach deliverance to the captives, and recovering of sight to the blind, to set at liberty them that are bruised." Jesus came to save us, but He also came to deliver us. It has been stated by many Christians that they were saved, but some of them stated also that they knew they needed to be delivered. The truth of the matter is that if we are claiming the Lord

Jesus and still acting and reacting in negative ways, then we need to be healed. What you want to remember is that internalizing your problems will definitely make you sick. People may not know that you have been hiding everything inside as a way to cope with your problems, but you know it's there, and so does the Lord. Internalizing problems is a reality, and if we ask the Lord, He will surely help us and heal us.

Study.com reveals what internalizing behaviors are: "Internalizing behaviors are behaviors that result from negativity that is focused inward." People with internalizing behaviors have difficulty coping with negative emotions or stressful situations, so they direct their feelings inside. Because everything is going on inside, "internalizing behaviors are usually not visible to others."

A few examples of internalizing behaviors are:

1. Social withdrawal
2. Loneliness or guilt
3. Sadness
4. Fearfulness

Putting It All Together:

1. What new habits can I start practicing that will help me avoid internalizing my problems?
2. Why does internalizing make you sick?
3. What scripture(s) can we meditate on to focus on healing?
4. Do believers sometimes internalize?

Conclusion

Start thinking about yourself in positive ways. You may not see it now, but you are important to God, and you will be who He called you to be as long as you don't quit. This is what the psalmist says in Ps. 139:14: "I will praise thee; for I am fearfully and wonderfully made." The psalmist believed that the Lord loved him and that he was important to Him.

If our old way of thinking hasn't worked out in so many years, it's definitely time for a change. I went through this for decades and decided that I needed a change, a better life, a life of peace and joy. I was introduced to the Lord Jesus

Christ on August 11, 1978. I accepted Him into my life, and it was the greatest thing that ever happened to me. Immediately, I had a mind to turn to my Heavenly Father. I began to learn how to pray, and I saw things in the Word of God that showed me how He could help me get through my problems. As I read the scriptures, I believed them; every time I needed Him, He was there to strengthen me. I'm so grateful that I didn't quit. Troubles don't always start in adulthood; they started with me when I was a child. I believe the devil knows those of us who belong to God, because the Bible says so in 2 Tim. 2:19 : "The Lord knoweth them that are His." The enemy the devil tries to destroy us while we are young because he knows that God has a plan for our lives.

Here are a few clips from my testimony:

After graduating from high school, I married at age nineteen. Neither my husband nor I knew anything about maintaining a marriage. It was

CONCLUSION

very hard, and we had lots of trials and errors, but by a miracle we survived fifty-four years of marriage. God blessed us with four beautiful children that gave a reason to live, and they all prospered in the way of the Lord.

Later in life the Lord led me to enroll in Bible college, and I stayed there until I received a Master's Degree in Christian counseling. The Lord led me back to Bible college in 2016, after I lost my mom. I needed an outlet, and it was very good for me. In 2018 I received a Doctorate Degree in Christian counseling at the age of seventy years old.

Today I'm almost seventy-four years old, and I know that I've made it this far in life because I didn't give up on myself and learned to quit stumbling over myself by taking personal responsibility for my actions and reactions to negative situations.

I understand, now more than ever, that most of the time, it's the decisions we make in our lives that determine whether we rise or fall. It's never too late for us to fix ourselves.

When we don't take personal responsibility for our actions and reactions in life and instead blame other people, we stumble over ourselves. It doesn't make a difference if it's a wall that we put up to withdraw ourselves because we don't want to be bothered or if we shut down and retreat to an emotional island to be by ourselves; negative speaking and thinking about ourselves will eventually destroy us. All of these negative events that we so often encounter can change and turn around if we allow it to happen. In Christ Jesus all things are possible to them that believe: "And He said, the things which are impossible with men are possible with God" (Luke 18:27). Whatever we need, He is the answer. He loves you, and if you turn to Him, He will make you a new creature: "Therefore if any man be in Christ, he is a new creature: old things are passed away; behold, all things are become new" (2 Cor. 5:17).

Don't struggle alone. You can always turn to the Lord because there is no problem too difficult for Him, and He welcomes all who come to Him. The ultimate goal for us in this life is to be saved, healed, and delivered and to show others the way.

About the Author

Dr. Ruby J. Harvey is the assistant pastor of Ebenezer Christian Assembly in Saint Louis, Missouri, where she works diligently in ministry with her husband, Pastor L. J. Harvey. In 1996 Dr. Harvey founded ICAM (I Care About Myself) Ministries, a ministry centered around helping people with low self-esteem, inner hurts, pain from the past, and much more. Many people have been delivered through this ministry.

Dr. Harvey has been preaching and teaching the Word of God for over forty-one years. She obtained a Master's Degree in Christian counseling from International Bible College and a Doctorate Degree from Saints Academy Bible College. Currently, she resides with her family in Saint Louis, Missouri, and is involved in outreach and Christian growth ministries.

Facebook: Ruby Harvey Ministries
Email: drrubyjay@gmail.com
www.drrubyharvey.com
Phone: (314) 418-9621

www.ingramcontent.com/pod-product-compliance
Lightning Source LLC
LaVergne TN
LVHW021304080526
838199LV00090B/6015